Six Mile Mountain

Six Mile Mountain

poems

Richard Tillinghast

Story Line Press | *Pasadena, CA*

ISBN 978-1-58654-112-5 (tradepaper)
978-1-58654-113-2 (casebound)

The National Endowment for the Arts, the Los Angeles County Arts Commission, the
Ahmanson Foundation, the Dwight Stuart Youth Fund, the Max Factor Family Foun-
dation, the Pasadena Tournament of Roses Foundation, the Pasadena Arts & Culture
Commission and the City of Pasadena Cultural Affairs Division, the City of Los Ange-
les Department of Cultural Affairs, the Audrey & Sydney Irmas Charitable Foundation,
the Kinder Morgan Foundation, the Meta & George Rosenberg Foundation, the Aller-
gan Foundation, the Riordan Foundation, Amazon Literary Partnership, and the Mara
W. Breech Foundation partially support Red Hen Press.

Second Edition
Published by Story Line Press
an imprint of Red Hen Press
www.redhen.org

Acknowledgments

Agni: "Sight" & "The Emigrant"

The American Voice: "Ever" & "The World Is"

The Boston Phoenix: "Opera on Jukebox"

Five Points: "Petition"

The Gettysburg Review: "Incident," "A Morning" & "Solstice"

The Hudson Review: "Currency"

The Kenyon Review: "Tea"

Michigan Quarterly Review: "Something by Vivaldi"

The Nation: "Six Mile Mountain"

The New Criterion: "The Alley Behind Ocean Drive," "Bijou and Majestic," "Exilium," "McLeod House," & "Work Station"

New England Review: "Habitat" & "The Red Cottage"

The New Republic: "Father in October," "Hooded Crow and Speedwell," & "Rain"

The New Yorker: "His Days"

Notre Dame Review: "Coming To"

Paris Review: "Starfuckers"

Partisan Review: "A Visit"

Ploughshares: "Westbound"

Poetry: "Wake Me in South Galway"

Poetry East: "Lexicons"

Shenandoah: "My Father's Glen Plaid Jacket"

Slate: "Am I Like a Tree"

The Southern Review: "A Box of Rain," "Departure" & "Wireless" Southwest Review: "On a Black-Market Icon of the Archangel Michael"

"Tea" was published in *A Visit to the Gallery: Poets Explore the Museum of Art*, ed. Richard Tillinghast, University of Michigan Press, 1997. "Father in October" & "Six Mile Mountain" appeared in *Home Works: A Book of Tennessee Writers*, University of Tennessee Press, 1996. "Rain" & "We Kept Missing Each Other" were included in *The Made Thing: An Anthology of Contemporary Southern Poetry*, ed. Leon Stokesbury, University of Arkansas Press, 1999. "Currency," "Lexicons," & "The World Is" also appeared in *The Lake George Arts Project Literary Review*, 1995.

This book is dedicated with love to my daughter,
Julia Clare Tillinghast

Contents

Six Mile Mountain

His Days

When one of his black moods bedeviled him,
When the wince of some remembered pain—
Some wrong done to him, some cruelty of his own—
Hurt him like a surge melting down
Bad wiring, what choice was left to him
But to flinch and swallow and bear it like a man?

The cottage's slates and silences became
His kingdom, its weathers his own. He would coax
To a blaze coal and turfs each morning, and chunks
Of beech he split with his own axe.
The farmer's son or Sunday hikers would see him
Hunched at his kitchen table, away in his books.

Then obscurely one morning he'd lock his cottage door.
With a word to no one he'd be gone,
To look at an old church somewhere, or the ruin
Of a tower down a dirt track, or a stone
Incised with markings no one could decipher,
Its language crumbling by degrees in the rain.

He could navigate the old script. And he knew why an arch
Was rounded or gothic. Why the mermaid
Held a mirror. Which sins the monks allowed
Themselves, and which they disavowed.
He knew the griefs of the high kings, belonged to the church
Of bitterness, had bet on the cards of pride.

But when on some grimy market town's main street
He heard a child, eyes widening in wonder,
Call out "Daddy!", reaching for his father,
It cut him like the crack of leather.
Then, it seemed, the pain was complete.
The water was wide, and he could not swim over.

A Visit

Mud spattered the windscreen of my rental car.
When I asked where she was buried, a memory fell
Like shade across the face of the woman who lived
In what had been the gate lodge—then a smile,
A shy welcome, and she pointed the way to the churchyard.
Then a child called her, so there was not a soul

Between me and the sand-blasted spire of the Protestant church.
The shape of her headstone, beveled like the gable
Of a Dutch canal-house, was, like her handwriting,
Charactered but unobtrusive. The lichened marble
Put me in mind of the mottled green Parker with which
She used to write. The doll's-house of a school

Stood out from the choir of the church, where Joseph in his coat
Of many colors was first betrayed, where Mary
"Kept all these things and pondered them in her heart."
I peered into those depths, through cobwebbed glass
Where desks swam in the green of a river twilight.
Thumbtacked to the wall was a snapshot of her house,

Gone now, and the print of a Pre-Raphaelite
Madonna and child. My neglect—I had let her grow old!—
Burned in my face, acknowledged now for the first time.
She was Mary in the painting, I was the child—
I could see that now—nurtured and wondered at.
Ungrateful, and leaving already, I had struggled

To step off into an air beyond her containment.
Nothing stirred in that churchyard, or gave the slightest impression
Her story and mine impinged on the afternoon.
I turned away, walked back to my car—
Warned off by a treeful of rooks—and drove out the gate.
How long it takes us to become who we are!

Ever

And when she was gone
the silver lost its frail brilliance,
the cut glass cobwebbed,
the clocks wound down.

The two brothers
in the story she would read us on Christmas Eve
never made their way in from the blizzard,
never rescued the beggar- woman from the snowdrift
or laid their pennies on the altar,
or found out why the chimes rang.

Father in October

for Brownie and Kate

When the smell of freshly sharpened pencils had lost
Its power to intoxicate, when our first
Infatuation with September had slackened—
With its satchels and homework and new teacher;
When the leaves of the late-blooming chrysanthemums
In our frost-finished back garden had blackened,
One morning my mother would retrieve our winter
Hats and scarves, our gloves and heavy raingear.
My father would go up attic, bring down the storms
And snug them in, between ourselves and the weather.

One hundred years of our family had lived
Beneath that house's airy ceilings, had sat
By a grate where coal sputtered and glowed in the glass
Cases where my grandfather's books were shelved—
Shakespeare, the Bröntes, Dickens, Sir Walter Scott.
And the house told stories, of interest only to us:
The well, sealed after Uncle John drowned a cat.
The deep-cut initials my older brother carved
Above the stairs. The bed my mother was born in.
Every dip in the floorboards spoke, every curious stain

Remembered. To marry my mother, my father found
In 1932, was to husband her house.
Its *fin de siècle* wiring was a fireman's nightmare;
What was airy in June was drafty in December.
"Manage," "Simplify," his granite New England
Eyes said. Those Willifords must have seemed another
Species altogether—with their Southernness,
Their leaky roof, their Eastlake furniture.
There was hardly a marble-topped table that didn't wobble,
Or a chair that couldn't have used some glue or a nail.

Saturdays he'd be up by six. First
A shave, and with his shaving brush he'd soap
Clean the lenses of his gold-rimmed glasses.
Then he'd collect himself over coffee and make a list,
Numbered and neat, of his day's projects in the shop
He had built out back under the hickory trees.
A nimbus of sawdust surrounding his concentration,
He'd turn a chair-leg on his lathe, cut out
A bracket or brace with his jigsaw, then fashion
A toy pistol for me, or a paddle-wheel boat.

Daddy's real work was engineering. His own
Dreams and epiphanies came to him, I imagine,
In the language of his calling—straightedged and clear
As a blueprint, verifiable by time and motion
Studies. His few inventions that made a profit,
The many he drew in his mind but had to give
Up on, lived a life pristine and platonic—
Not subject to half-measures or the change of season,
Not battered by weather or in need of repair
Like the mortal house I judged him master of.

Hooded Crow and Speedwell

His unblinking coal-chunk eye awake
To carrion or a young nestling fallen
His way, that self-possessed hooded fellow
Hops on the chimney-stack, ready to lurch
Out on the leathery menace of his wing-stroke.

Dream-bothered, up before the farmers,
I hunch by the fire and watch him. At lambing time
The herdsmen blast away at the crow, or throw stones.
He swoops at their shaky wool-fluff heartbeats.
Have a care for the baby. Keep the kitten indoors.

The same day, out walking, not so much to get
Anywhere as to wipe from my feet the reprimand
Of the grave I stood by in my dream, I am buoyed
Up by swells of buttercups, startled by wild orchids.
Then a downpour soaks me before I can find that

Bright-eyed blue I needed, growing
Threaded into a hedge: rained-on glances
Of speedwell—blue as the sky I wished for, purpling
To gloaming, no bigger than a baby's tooth. Why
Have I walked a mile to find it? What is it saying?

Rain

The rain, the incessant drench,
　　　　the lap of it puddling up,
　　　　　　　　seen through spattered window glass.
And all of us in that long house together
　　　　where all the talk was of the weather,
　　　　house-partying on a rainy weekend.

Fragrance of toast, incessant cups of tea.
The wind mulled and hovered,
　　　　　the wind set all the buttercups in the field a-tremble.
I would sit all morning in the blue armchair transfixed,
　　　　hearing the whoosh and settle of wind and rain
　　　surround and define
　　　　the astral shape of the cottage.

The rain was sleep till half past ten,
the rain was not having to shave,
the rain was opium,
the rain was an ocean voyage through blackness.
The rain was a whisper under coverlets,
　　　a barely moving lace between us and the trees.
The rain was constant, sempiternal, older than woodsmoke.

And then it would bow its head and subside,
　　　and a blackbird
tuning cleanly pinnacles of delight from a dry perch
　　　　　　under dripping boughs
would put you in mind
of Noah and his lot
　　　drifting becalmed when the waters retreated.

I wanted it never to end,
I wanted to deconstitute and emanate out
        beyond the force-field of the cottage
    like lamplight through wet windows,
            and let the rain possess me entirely—
        let it soak right down
            into the pores of my happiness.

The World Is

The world is a man with big hands
and a mouth full of teeth.
The world is a ton of bricks, a busy signal,
your contempt for my small talk.
It's the crispy lace that hardens
around the egg you fry each morning
sunny side up.

The world is the last week of August,
the fumes that dizzy up into the heat
when you fill your tank
on the way to work late, again.
The world is "Please take a seat over there."
The world is "It'll have to come out."
The world is "Have a nice day."

The world is "What is that peculiar smell?"
The world is the button that popped off,
the watch that stopped, the lump you discover and
                    turn on the light.
The world is a full ashtray, the world is that grey look,
the world is the County Coroner of Shelby County.
The world is a cortège of limousines,
an old man edging the grass from around a stone.

The world is "Belfast Says No!", the world is reliable
sources, a loud bang and shattered glass raining down
                    on shoppers.
The world is a severed arm in a box of cabbages, "And then
the second bomb went off and we didn't know which
way to run." The world is Semtex and black balaclavas
and mouth-to-mouth resuscitation. The world is
car alarms silenced, and a street suddenly empty.

The world is one thousand dead today in the camps.
The world is sixty thousand latrines, the world is
bulldozers pushing bodies and parts of bodies into a ditch.
The world is dysentery and cholera,
infected blood, and vomit. The world
is mortality rates and rape as an instrument of war.
    The world
is a 12-year-old with an iPhone, a can of Coke, and an Uzi.

The Alley Behind Ocean Drive

On beach sand two thousand footprints
Cross and overlay
And form or seem to form a pattern.
Girls speaking Italian
Take off their tops
And breathe the sun in through their pores.

The sun sets gorgeously
And then the *jeunesse dorée*, or
Eurotrash as they are called locally,
Drift back to their suites to change.
Then they emanate out onto Ocean Drive,
Sherbet- colored, to please the night air.

Behind Ocean Drive and the Colony Hotel
Runs an alley, unnamed,
Where Cuba comes to work.
When someone in the grill orders in English
The dishes get shouted
Out through the kitchen in Spanish.

People come here from far away
To spend money. Behind the Imperial,
In the alley, someone chops ice, fish are gutted,
Dirt gets washed off roots.
The ditch that runs down the
Middle of it runs red.

Out on Ocean the guy with the parrot angles for tips,
Madame Amnesia deals out a Tarot hand,
Iguana-on-a- bicycle lady wobbles
Amongst the Eurotrash. I write
My page, my way is paid.
All of us ride the swell of a tide.

The offal, the scales, the T-bones from steaks,
The hearts and lemon rinds, are put in bags
That the city comes by and collects.
Two towels hang on a balcony overlooking the alley.
A man in a white apron
Stands outside alone and smokes.

Starfuckers

"Isn't it time I slipped my leash?"
      she thought. For him, what was it?
A quickening. A corner he hadn't turned.

Their hands, their eyes, their mouths,
          each discreet designer bruise,
pronounced each other's body canonical.

While at the same time knowing
      love is the sublimest form of stupidity,
they looked into each other's
eyes as if refining the expression
          on a self-portrait.

The way she formed her letters made his breath catch.
The postman was a chubby little cupid.

They were both
      starfuckers.

"Your lower lip drives me wild,"
    she said
        in a trattoria.

Wireless

Anchorite of insomnia,
3 AM exile thumbing a skyful
Of shortwave radio
Static, through unidentifiable
Squiggles and blurted Morse, I nudge the dial
Millimeter by millimeter
Across a spatter

Of languages—three different Englishes— Goldberg
variations, a hemisphere's
Weather and news flashes,
While a gale off the North Atlantic tears
At my island's landward moorings, and roars
Through every frequency
In the crackling sky.

Only a thread keeps me from slipping
Anchor, from floating like an imaginary
Iceberg out to sea, sleeping
Toward Greenland, or adrift entirely—
Unmoored beyond these signals, this rosary
Of stations. A finger's touch
Keeps me attached.

McLeod House:
Poem Ending In A Line By Milton

Imagine turbines at full roar,
Steel particles sparking, lit up by fluorescent tubes
Above an assembly line.
A machinist smoking, biceps tattooed, rebuilding a jet engine.
A farmer pulling stumps out of bottomland
With a mule and log-chain in the rain.
Or someone wringing a mop
Out, preparatory to swabbing a dining hall floor.

Then think of this place and day:
Maples stippled with the first ambers and scarlets,
Chilled air into which sunlight
Does not force itself
But instills or decants.

McLeod House—a mustard yellow clapboard mansion
With scrolled Ionic capitals and fluted columns—
Will have been pointed out
On your tour of the university.
Inside, smell beeswax, pipe tobacco, ink.

Before Independence, craftsmen whose descendants
Sail yachts now, mitered oak for wainscoting, planed down
Planks of white pine from the king's forests in New Hampshire,
Sawed and hammered, plumbed and plastered; and then
In the twenties some threadbare survivor
Of a mercantile family with clippers east to Japan
Willed to Harvard this variorum of substance and labor.

Climb three dizzy flights, boards creaking underfoot
To a cell just wide enough to swing a cat in,
Which once roofed the dreams of Mary or Bridget
From the bogs of Connemara, who cried at night
And cabled dollars to the home she wouldn't see again.

The current tenant lays a Dickensian fire in the grate,
Marks bluebooks, and daydreams while surfing the net
Of writing what the *Times* will call "the definitive
History of the iamb." Until then he annotates bibliographies,
And leaves fall like footnotes over Quincy Street.
Where else but McLeod House to take one's stand,
      filled with resolve
To scorn delights, and live laborious days?

My Father's Glen Plaid Jacket

That bias-cut seam around the collar
has come unstitched now.
The label says Oak Hall, Memphis.
Its oak clusters evoke
a banqueting hall and woodsmoke of Englishness.
But it's my Dad's jacket.
His sweat must still be somewhere in the satin lining.

I wear the thousand times he put it on
to drink old-fashioneds,
or to go to the theatre,
and I can see him in it at the railing
as some bargain cruise ship left for South America.
But mostly when he put it on to go to church.

I wear it and try to be true
and oaklike, as he was,
knowing that while God's kingdom
might come
and His will might be done
on earth as it is in Heaven,
whether or not we can quite follow it—

As for the likes of my Dad and me, we
sweated in a white collar for our daily bread
and tried to live within the boundaries
set by our trespasses
asking not to be led into temptation—
working, putting money in the bank,
kneeling to pray
while unceasingly, mysteriously
moved around us
the kingdom, the power, the glory.

Work Station

As if mentally punching a time clock
which rings with triggered, impersonal resolution,
I crouch to some task, adhere to a list, and check
items off, releasing the sudden out-thrown
breath that says "Now, *that's* done!"

With every ordering, each neatness—
dust waxed from a surface, a long overdue letter
written and faxed—snow accumulates,
clocks tick. I scissor stems, put roots in a jar,
advance pale rootlets into the future.

Then suddenly feathered, crest-risen, I peer down
at my turtle's inch from the blue sky's vantage point,
eavesdropping on the man at my work station
as I check my messages or run a word count,
evolved to the level of an ant.

Ever again, will jonquils or poetry break
the crust of these well-scrubbed quotidian
satisfactions? When will I read, unassigned, a book
Again? Loft a dry fly, drift on breezes that quicken?
Give up all effort—and awaken?

A Morning

Knowing the answer or not
knowing the answer,
penciling the morning in,
staring right back at the egg yolks
while the baby crawls on the rug.
Watching the last day of August
transpire, with its sharp, peculiar light.

Working for the department, changing
a tire, letting the phone ring.
Innocent, truly not knowing
the answer,
honestly holding no opinion.
Seventy-four degrees exactly.

The ordinariness of it,
I suppose, was what struck the Buddha,
camped out along the road to awakening
as he watched the moment ignite,
incinerate, and disperse.

Departure

What is this lightness I can't define,
that rises like river mist
over everything the eye beholds?

A life's narratives
stack up.
Twenty-five years ago I left someone's bed with a headache,
waking to gusty 5 AM on Riverside Drive,
and crossed the George Washington Bridge,
compass oscillating south and west

with an absorption in the moment
as in an old churchyard—
where everything of note, everything that has gone wrong,
is assuaged by alphabets of mosses;
where the yew trees, older than horticulture,
drink the returns of the seven seas.

The road was the only way to go.

Even as I transit the defeated landscape
that buys and sells, that smiles and photosynthesizes
within fallout range of the city,
the ornamentals do their thing
punctually, like sparkling burgundy
at Auld Lang Syne time.

Soon we die, and all this is past,
but today I sit in the driver's seat
and drive,

the map spread out on the seat beside me,
continuous airy streams of noise paralleling me—
layered horizontals of internal combustion,
rubber over asphalt,
RPMs detonating pastel smog.

Willows open like a door
into some green inner layer of existence.
One more year I'm alive to see these buds
gladden the May woods.

My throttle opens up.
I feel my tendons stretch as the gears shift,
moving out over blue sky-mirages
and roadkill spangled over the pavement,
a breeze feathering the fur
of those not fast enough in crossing.

Eight days on the road
through the poetry of radio guitars,
past the styrofoam leavings of America,
I'm passing everything in sight,
pursuing the methodical achievement of distance
into the ink-wash of a thundery sky.

A Box Of Rain

You lit out from Reno, you were trailed by twenty hounds.
And yet it's hard to think of you gone

because I keep seeing you out of the corner of my eye
passing through the back roads of Marin in a '52 Chevy
and then up into Sonoma,
laying low in a motel in Novato or Petaluma,
taking your time leaving.

I hear gone notes
through the incorporeality of your guitar,
cool like the shade under redwoods.

You stand isolated on stage
and enter the melody and leave it
as a cyclist veers and lays back
around corners, along streets in the rain.

I'm listening. I've got American Beauty
on my front porch cranked up real loud
while a crew tears the roof off
across the street from me.

You were Jerry Garcia, you were Captain Trips
and later an apologetic looking big furry cat
who looked like he slept in his clothes,

an open and closed book of life
in that realm
where all the print is blood
and our names are for a time.

For you the petals have all unfolded.
"All the birds that were singing," you sang
"are flown except you alone." And now
you too are gone.

On A Black-Market Icon Of The Archangel Michael

Those eyes hard as black agates opened
Once—in light that ushered into vision
Fluted epiphanies of Doric marble
        Standing like bleached pine masts,

Cobalt depths breaking white on immovable
Stone, that an angel somehow rolled away.
Eyes fixed on a man shaking off the stinking
        Dirt of the grave.

Eyes whose inwardness held the burned
Knowledge of Alexandria's shelves.
Opened once and stayed open. I walk
        This morning from my Levantine

Hotel through bazaar light storied with dust
Of exhausted empire. Propped and mortgaged and treatied,
It crashed—a Viennese piano pushed
        From the final floor of a palace.

Through that lingering astral chord,
Through a clatter of smithies, I walk out of the light
Under shadows of domes, into a beehived maze
        Of disputatious lanes

And sit cross-legged on the woven traditions
Of nomads, to construct with a melancholy smoker
An architecture of numbers, and strike a bargain
        For this archangel's gaze.

Someone stowed adrenaline, flight, the sight of
A torched basilica, into his saddlebag
And galloped the icon across a fiery horizon.
        Propped on my hotel dresser

Michael heartens me. He has drawn his sword
And stands to defend me against all
Blunt minds, all who buy and sell,
    All who have made their peace with time.

Currency

No bed for me in this city tonight, no key
in my pocket for anyone's door.
No cure for the rain
that revives the dusty quayside sycamores
and wears away the faces
on statues of the famous dead.

Decades gone, I'd amble these quays,
jingling the harps and salmons and peacocks in my pockets,
my sense of pure form freshened
by vertical parallels of 18th-century brick
that stripe the currents of rippled dull jade
careering down to the sea
between banked, peeling trunks
of river-drinking trees.

I must have blinked, though,
because now two girdered cranes,
one immemorial blue, one summer-camp green,
wrecking the lovely city brick by brick,
wheel in a cluttered sky
as weepy as the sad watercolors
my dead aunt used to paint.

The key changes, clouds modulate, sunshine
recurs. My footsteps
evanesce from the cobblestones.

Sight

My left quadrant of vision,
eyesight laid unfocusedly across a floor of rough tiles,
fetches up against
a rectangle of terra-cotta chimney
faced along its right edge by a vertical board,
while a stovepipe elbows up the center of the bricks.

My right eye
looks out streaky glass bisected horizontally
by a shelf varnished the color of chestnuts,
six feet through to a blue wall
with mallows legging up like kisses through the space between,
and a peat-lined hanging basket of lobelia—
mood indigo with bright-white centers,
topped by magenta petunias

and something precise and scarlet I don't recognize.
A laundry line yellow as a slicker
cuts off-horizontally
across the off-vertical slant of the mallows.

Swallows, their pendant tails flicking like snakes' tongues,
rest on phone lines that sag, as well,
in the northcoast sky's saturation—
close to white, underlaid with blue—
then veer, dart and accelerate,
scissor and swerve.

On the radio someone sings "I only have eyes
for you"—
restoring my faith in symmetry.

Habitat

Shine your light between the stones here:
a tortoiseshell butterfly, isn't it?—
holed up like the rest of the self-renewing world this February day
     with only us out for a walk.

Its wingtips serrate like the lip of a seashell—
     patterned dabs, dusky as the clove-stuck orange in the parlor,
like ashtray burns, brown centering to black.

I know if I take one of this butterfly's wings
     between the thumb and forefinger of each of my hands
and explicate it like a doll's fan
I can show you the big black ink-swabs
     topping each powdery wing, like single strokes of midnight.

But my hands are not sunshine.
     Leave the tortoiseshell,
       like a spare pair of spectacles,
folded in its crevice with eight or ten others
     in the wall of this fortified tower that half stands

     on a rise in a pasture.
Its top storeys fell, or were battered and tumbled
     downhill into a tarn, and
I don't even know where to put my hand
on the book that would tell us what baron
or cattle-thieving chieftain or shrewd abbot built it
     in which dark century, or in which campaign he lost it,

abandoning the position
to colonies of mosses and lichens, cow patties,
the rusted-out door of an old Morris
     propped against the wall.

A long-eared bat, *plecotus auritus*, stirs
     and propels itself out of hibernation.
Its amazing ears stand out from its head
and it looks like a hyper-vitamined rabbit
     as it navigates its goofy flight-jags
       on wings of parchment.

Over our heads where he errs, there's a clear view—
     no ceiling left after five hundred years—
to a huge untidy bundle of kindling
     lodged above a fireplace big enough
       to roast two sheep in.
A raven on nest creaks her settled wings and croaks down at us.

       The male deploys in a lancet window, a
choker of sable ruffed about his neck.
     His beak makes him feudal, sub rosa, henchman—
outwardly a study in resignation,
       but versed in the code of duello.

Ravens lay their eggs in February—
       think of the caution of it.
No flowers bloom yet, of any kind, to line their
     unassailable nest. Certainly not!

Legends Of Lady Fitzpigge-Hightits

Did God in one of his wilder flights of fancy
Ever make a woman—no matter how hard she might
Ride to hounds, no matter with how sure a hand
Skipper a yacht through gale-whipped seas, or fill
A ball gown to perfection—who could hold a candle
To Lady Hightits?

        Mornings, when I heard skirts glide
Past my schoolroom door, I'd creep out into the hall
To obsequiate and pull my forelock, leaving
The little viscounts to their hic-haec-hocs,
Shutting the door on that olfactorium
Of ink and library paste and porridge farts—

To breathe Mount FitzPigge's wider freedoms, its air
Of cut flowers and beeswax and China tea,
And Lady Foxglove's famous *potpourris*.
She'd brisk along with her plaid-kilted secretary
Beside her, jotting down notes, her English butler
Sniffing along behind, the Pekineses nipping his spats.

The things they did with their money! (most of it
From coal mines in South Wales, mind you, no matter
How many unicorns or griffins or wyverns
Quartered or pranced or buggered across their coat
Of arms).

        Fancy their building their own airfield—
Lady Windrush-Libertyscarf buzzing the lough
In her Gypsy-One
Moth, Lord Stablecock buggering off
To surprise one of his actresses, or swooping
Down to Gstaad to fetch the little snotnoses
Home from skiing, in his Percival Q6
Six-seater.

Four chauffeurs for four cars! Not
To mention his-and-her Rollses. And the house
Packed out with guests—Vita Sackville-West
And that wet husband of hers in his stiff tweeds,
Yeats with his *pince-nez* and fluttering hands and dandruff,
Gobbling scones and ringing for endless cups of tea,
John Betjeman fogging his glasses over the Georgian brasswork.

Me, with my Trinity B.A. and my book
Of eclogues from Skylark Press—for afternoon tea
It was ironstone crockery and broken meats
In the servants' kitchen, the conversational arts
Of the pimply telegraph boy and under-house
Parlourmaid, wet boots, and a whiff of petrol
Off the chauffeur's tunic—except when the literary crowd
Came round, and nobody else could speak their language.

Today the Rollses have fetched up in vintage
Car collections, the house in Park Lane demolished,
An hotel put up in its place, the 12th Marquess
Ambushed on the coast road by the IRA.

But when Lady Hightits stood tiara'd at the top
Of those marble stairs, translucent as alabaster,
Receiving with the Prince of Wales on one side,
The Viceroy on the other (I lurked behind
The gladioli in a dinner jacket borrowed
From Lord Quickflask), her black-and-silver
Sequined bosom—*beaucoup du monde au balcon*—
Seemed designed by evolution and Burke's Peerage
To dazzle the world's eyes with the FitzPigge diamonds.
Every gesture of her hands flashed wristful of sapphires.
Her dress glittered like a coat of mail. She attacked
Like a young Crusader suited up for battle.

Lexicons

Search parties, ice-axed, cramponed: dispatched
    into the unfrequented high-country
        of my mental thesaurus
to pin an unthumbed word
    on the uncoined cry of
this coot I'm watching,
        who coasts among
    lily pads where she has splashed down,
        churning up metaphors.

Her vocalized monosyllable
        can't be the eponymous "Coot!"
proposed by my bird book—
but something closer to a high-register "Squinx!"
    as absurd officious *Fulica atra*
cruises the lake hegemonically, like a toy gunboat,
        dependencies in tow.

As we drift, as we navigate and divagate—
the coot and I—
        a pointy-eared red squirrel
scurries overhead up the *pinus radiata*
           I'm leaning against,
    and cries in alarmed contralto
        like one-inch-wide expensive grosgrain
yanked very fast, singing,
        off a milliner's cardboard spool.

The Emigrant

Two places only
there were:
here and America.
The four corners of the farm,
and gone-beyond-the-sea.

With a twopenny nail
he etched into the iron
shank of his spade
the word "Destiny,"
drove it with his boot smartly into the turf
and left it standing.

Abroad commenced
at the town line.
The New World blinded him
on the Navan road
and again the first time he tried to speak English
and again the first time he saw an orange.

Anesthetized by reels and barrels of porter
and eight renditions of "The Parting Glass,"
he fell asleep to the groan of oars
and awoke to a diesel thrust
and sleet over mountainous seas.

Coming To

The lookback is a troubled vista over
many turnings. The flight-jags of a raptor,
determined scrambles over demesne walls.
Compass readings, shivering, on a moor—
      the stars cutting like struck flint.

Arrival, and a muddle of memories.
      Long sleep, like a deep plunge.
Then to float in feathery repose,
dreams interlaved with the vowels of healers
who sat by your bed and spoke your name
as if from a distance, or in foreign syllables,
    cleansing your wounds with their voices.

Clinking of muffled crockery.
A place has been prepared for you, as if
by an unseen presence. Your shaving basin
steams by a west window where rain
      ticks and runs together coherently.

Wait, though. Who is that dusty man leaving,
      letting himself out the back gate?
A man in a black suit with bits
of straw in its weave and in his hair,
who looks like having slept in a ditch—
his face bricky, eyes bloodshot, like hedge wrens
    that dart away when you look at him straight.

Westbound

First a startle of fragrances
to remind me where I am:
turf smoke blown through drizzle,
oystery brine-tang over Quay Street.

An umbrella-raking gale.
Then mind-blowing blue above the town for a nanosecond
    until my airport-bound rented windscreen
spatters with the weather's wet
        splash of anticipation and
by an astral lope I'm back in a place with trees where

I picture you holding open a Victorian door shyly—
    then an almost imperceptible bouquet
        of lavender and myrrh
        from between your thighs.

Two virtues of a Catholic girlhood:
the name Mary, and secrets in the dark.

This far away I can touch the hard nubby stars
of chrysanthemums that I put in the ground,
        watered and husbanded. They bud up now.

        Petit Sirah
and, as a present for you, notecards
    with Kilkenny rooks
        settling among smoky chimney-stacks and
            copper beeches.

But how can I write on flat paper
this impulse that arcs between us, inarticulately,
        as I fly?

Opera On Jukebox

Caffè Trieste, San Francisco

"*Un Bel Dì Vedremo*" finishes
and then "*Una Furtiva Lacrima*"
swallow-tails through the café
recasting tobacco walls as tiers of boxes
like the bosoms of the convent school's senior class
lined up in presentation mode for the big evening out.
The soprano's semi-quavers dagger
Neapolitan bedchamber velvets,
and the blood of cousins flows.

This the music must accomplish
to the accompaniment of two massive exhaust fans
stirring a power of roasted coffee beans.
Out high transom windows one glimpses two flags—
ours, and the Italian tricolor's vertical stripes:
white like the clouds against which it appears,
green like malice, red like the heart
as it empties and fills.

Tea

Erase a statue of Buddha, eyes lidded on nonexistence.
Erase topiary.
Take away red paint and gilding if you can.

This is a place to sit for a while,
the mats fresh,
smell of rain in rushes.

A crane glides without moving its wings
over the stream's length.
Peonies bloom in silk.

Is the stream a part of nature, or has it been
altered by the sages?
A shower blows up among cypresses up trail.

The tea master is away.
Otherwise how should I be here?

Over foothills scrolling,
mist brightens and evanesces.
Families of monkeys move over the ridge above,
through jungle, mist frozen on their muzzles.

Brown smoke from cooking fires
finds a path up here
from where the nomads camp.
God knows what they are burning.

Then the clear green tea:
green like water at the bottom of the ocean,
but hot as a bowl of soup.

Behind us, the trek over the mountains,
hand-drawn maps, bad knees and brambles.

Who knows what thundery warlord or dakini
caused the wind to blow the clouds
from one side of the mountain to the other?

Where the trail switchbacks above us, two
immortals play at chess.

Osmanca

The parade-ground elegance of her conjugations
thickened my tongue.
Her declensions were a *corps de ballet.*

Bearing in our thorn-cut hands
roses to place on the grave of an infant
we ascended, foot-wobbly from hours in her bed,
flights of stairs jungled in jasmine,
shattered in the War of Independence—
through an acre of yew trees, marble turbans snapped off their shafts,
sculpted Aeolian harps, conquered Paschal lambs.

Apexing, next morning, the iron filigree bridge
between her Europe and her Asia
I would sigh upward into the Iznik of a sky
four provinces Balkan,
six districts Mediterranean.

When my lips formed the possessive couplet—
her most characteristic construction—
my nostrils widened to a suggestion
part river-drinking plane trees, part sea-tang, part sunburned thyme.

Pronouncing her—even as poorly as I did—
sheathed me in the hauteur of vanished empire.

How could I return then
to the diphthongs and parataxis of my homeland?

Am I Like A Tree

planted by the water
in this congregation, in my father's glen plaid jacket?
What are these other
well-dressed communicants doing here?

My camel would balk at any attempt
to drive him through the eye of a needle.
What good would it do
to abandon my father and my mother,
now both gone anyway,
and give my worldly goods to be sold?

Yet I think I know what it means
to take up my cross daily.

What am I to make of this advice
to seek first the kingdom of Heaven?
The paths of righteousness
are brambled over, are they not?
Rocky, and the footing is bad.

Yet even I have sat down among stones
rough-hewn into blocks two cubits on a side,
and counted my money out in my hands
to see if I could pay to have my tower built.

Asters, I think it is,
on the altar. Someone has laundered and starched the cloth
and now it reflects whitely up onto the silver chalice
as I would expect it to do
at a luncheon in Heaven.

Though I may join my voice with angels and archangels
and all the company of Heaven, evermore praising
Thee and singing this hymn to proclaim the glory
of Thy holy name;
and though I may even be allowed sometimes
to drink the cup of salvation
and eat the bread of Heaven,
I could never really cut it
as a disciple.

Step sure-footedly.
Be a tree with roots.
Have money in your hand.
Kneel. Rejoice.

We all know one fine morning
we will be called on
in one breath
to renounce all that we have.

Petition

I was taught as a child about the kingdom
And the power, and the glory that overarches
Our little lives. And when my hard moment came
I prayed—that surely is the word—"Let me live."
I breathed that prayer out into a kindly sensate
Surround I could feel, a power I could touch,
If only in thought: an essence of the air
I breathed, which somehow cared for me, whether
I believed or understood—that wasn't the point.
"Let me live. Please. I have work to do."

When I thought "kingdom" I pictured a messenger,
The hooves of his ready pony pounding stones
Across a riverbed. A night of frost
And alarms. Under black pines, iron gates opened
To the king's hunting lodge up a mountain—
Letters to the court in his saddlebags,
My petition only one of many.
But it would be entered in the big ledger
And attended to in good time. I could picture
The broad nib of the scribe's pen scoring the fiber
Of the paper. "Let me live" was my petition,
"I have people who depend on me."

Glory I knew little about firsthand—
A high-raftered hall with a thousand beeswax candles
Blazing, glimpsed through mullioned windows.
I stood outside in the snow looking up
While the hard, faithful little fist of muscle
Inside my chest opened and closed, hammered
And hesitated, skipped and fluttered, praying.

Six Mile Mountain

The ground held more stones than dirt. No arrowheads,
No shaped flint-chips rose to their pick and shovel.
No one had disturbed these rocks since God and the glacier
Laid them down in anger.

They attacked the shelved-in limestone with their pick,
And flecks rained dryly down on dead oak leaves.
Dogwood misted the woods, forsythia brightened.
The stores in Six Mile were selling flowers for Easter.

Tears fell into the hole they were digging.
They sweated out last night's whiskey and grief.
In the high air's stillness that hard metallic ping
Ricocheted off tree trunks, bare and obdurate.

Finally the earth's coolness breathed up to them.
Little winged things flitted in the air above
The grave. Thumbnail-sized black butterflies appeared.
Black-capped chickadees perched on the black limbs

And answered the sharpened cries of pick and shovel.
The day warmed. Mare's-tails flared across the sky's
Bland cerulean. In the air-drifts
That skimmed the ridge a hawk glided, watching.

Solstice

An unaccustomed lightness,
like viola strings pizzicati.
Like a warbler's heart when it flutters.
A key of sunshine tumbles the
locked snowfields.

My delight skips over the gables' dazzle,
leaps with the eye's agility downhill
where the town keeps indoors.

Here and there on the roof of his house a man
shovels snow off.
Every chimney puffs its
definition of human life.

Bijou And Majestic

Snow from the first of November, snow
Darkening the already dark December
Sky over Montpelier. We stamped into the Bijou
Through slush, having nowhere to go other
Than my aunt's, or back to the farm. Images
Blizzarded through unfiltered smoke out of the
Fluttery projector's light-beam—
Hollywood soup for a twenty-below afternoon.

Satin flowed along Harlowe's thighs, men
In smoking jackets fingered cigarette holders,
B-29s droned low over Tokyo amid wet wool
Indoors-smells steaming in the stalls of the Bijou.

Out on the main street as evening closed in
We walked back together wrapped
In the full dark of the Green Mountains,
Haloed by our breath, upstairs to that little
Maid's room your job at the Majestic
Afforded you, and an iron bed with white sheets.

If I were still young and stupid enough
I would try to say
What we were to each other back then.

The Green Mountains whitened at the rim
Of our awakening, through a diamond-shaped window,
Its frame painted summer-camp green.

The Red Cottage

What we've called the red cottage
Since way back before we were follicly challenged
Is brown now. Burned down and rebuilt.
I can trudge upriver and fish at "the tractor seats"
But they were removed from the bank
When my boys were in Cub Scouts.

Blink, and I see an eerie burnishment
Like the sunset occluded, at midday:
The forest fire as it approached,
Burning the red cottage to the ground,
Sparing the lodge where we stay.
Our years there were not burned.

On Downriver Road the Mom & Pop
Is owned by a new mom & pop.
Along the banks, animal and fishermen's
Paths run, a badger's den of destinations.
It might be a plan of Paris
Four thousand years ago. Or the nascent grid of a metropolis
Next millennium, Dark Age streets hoof- and foot-beaten into the
      marsh,
Furtive little doglegs tunneled through tag alders and larch.

The Hendrickson hatch comes on in May, or else
It does not. Or else it does
And you are not in the river then,
Taking a nap or writing poetry or hunting morels.
Or else it rains, and only an undeterred diehard
Is out in a slicker, casting a green
Feather wrapped with sparkles,
Flashing it over gravelly shallows.

In the cottage you read obscure back numbers of *Field and Stream*
Or craft, on a fly-tying vise,
Hendricksons, trig as a sailboat,
Wings transparent as the lights of a Japanese teahouse,
White-and-brown hair of something, tufted—
Then the spinner, spent wings finished, sprawled out
Dead on the river that pours and pours downstream.

Exilium

The imperial city toward which all roads tend,
Which codifies the laws and dispatches them
By runner or fax to expectant provinces
This is not. It's an improvised mélange
Mushrooming along the banks of a tidal river,
Suffering the moods of its irrational weather
And a population with much to complain about.

Though you could dignify what draws you here
By calling it exile, your solitude is your choice,
Even when it racks you, even when
Your tendons stretch with what you have to carry.
Out you go tonight making the rounds, mapping
A route through the city's drizzly melancholia,
Down streets of broad colonial emptiness.

Step inside a stained-glass door or two
Where shag and porter cloud the conversation.
Sip a slow pint in the company of strangers
While outside the rain slurs through globed lamp-glow.
The evening ages. A notebook fills with your
Idiosyncratic alphabet. Then the pubs close.

The pubs close, the streets rain-slick and desultory.
A cafeteria then—everybody's
Hangout, where plain lives put in appearances
Over tea and a bun. The cash register whirrs,
The steamy rush of the coffee machine backgrounds
A clink of ironstone plates and stainless steel.
No sigh of leisure here—every life
In the room carries the imprint of having worked
The livelong day—not to boast or prove
A point, but simply because what else is there?

The way an old sufferer, grey hair wispy and thin,
Handles her knife, addressing a plate of fish,
Reaches you, touches some common chord.
Despite what they say about you—beyond your remoteness,
Your severe judgments on your fellow creatures—
You've some connection still to the human race.
Hypercritical, incommunicado,
It's good to know deep down you're one of us.

The Bacon

Attach one clamp to the negative pole of the dead battery,
Then the other to the plus pole of the live one,
Negative to negative, take it from there.
Smoke a Lucky Strike if you have one.

Break an egg into that hot grease.
Use the power drill, twist those lug nuts off clean.
Hold that person's hand.
Pull down the lever on the button machine.

Unlock the office door, turn the computer on
And get into Windows. Fasten the buckle.
Make a little trench to plant the seeds in.
Click on Word. Run the ball off tackle.

The Button

That button dangled:
threadwork of a spider
who had flunked her Home Ec. course.
My jacket, already a size too loose,
lagged off one shoulder
as if blown by an August wind.

Needle and thread I needed, sharpness
and extension, penetration and follow-through.
First bought a black pig-snout of a spool.
Then Sarah looked in the kitchen and found
in the third drawer down, her mother's needle—
unbending, a fairy pikestaff.

Outdoors, while swallows and house martins swooped
near enough to tell them apart—
treble twitter of the swallow from the dull "stirrup"
of the martin—I poked, slow-fingered seamster,
the snub needle nose through corduroy
and secured that errant discus of bone.

Then put the jacket on again,
drew together the two halves of my person,
fastened that essential button,
and walked off into what awaited.

Incident

I slept, dead to the world, then awoke.
My daughter stood at the foot of the bed
calling me to supper, her corn-stubble hair
dyed red in the sunset. The honest wells
of her eyes brimmed toward me. I was grateful.
My sleep had been summery and boatlike.

Nothing had stopped. My sheets were not marble,
the earthy savor of death did not surround me.
All it was, was a June afternoon and time
for supper. I lay in bed a moment longer
and studied the lifeline on my palm,
how it cut passionately into the flesh,
then jagged abruptly to one side
like a slantwise heartbeat.

I was dead no longer, I had come back
from that slow place, that backward-flowing river,
that acre of reticence. Now I had eyes
once more to see and perceive in this world.
It was "Hi, honey," "Hi, Dad" and "How was your nap?"—
corn on the cob and salad from the garden
and coffee in my favorite cup.

Something By Vivaldi

There's a word—there has to be, there always is,
But today I can't find it—for how the quotidian
Errand-running self gives legs to the leafy
Glistening part of us that now and again surfaces,
Transporting that breeze-like something with a pen
And notebook from a snug seat at the Norseman
One street back from the rain-bothered Liffey,
To a caneback rocker on the porch at Sewanee

Where oakleaf and birdsong stipple down breeze-blown
Onto the page you fill—to a sun-warmed rock beside
The Big Lost River where you set your fly rod down
And write. Or your improvised niche is this brick arcade
In Seattle, discovered not by design
And not exactly by chance, where a classical busker
Rosins up and tunes up and delights the air
With a dazzle of sixteenth notes under arches of rain.

The music scaffolds its ascent up an invisible
Peak, bouncing on swells like a yacht, cloud-bound—
Elaborating story-lines around an allegorical
Citadel, sky-blue roads cutting a spiral
Up the angle of Paradise, like an apple
Being peeled by an exacting and pleasure-loving hand,
By a hand that is itself no more than smoke.
Then it swings and plunges, and barrels along like a truck.

And all of us gasp and hum and sway
To this lightness that builds a room beyond
The bricks of the arcade, the fire in the pub grate,
The masonry, timber and commerce that build a street,
The force that cut the Big Lost River into granite
Or that puts a chair out on the porch in Tennessee.
All of us: lunching merchants, students, a blonde
Hippie in a Disneyland T-shirt, two out-of-whiskey

Greybeards on a bench; and your reporter,
Brought here for no other purpose than to get it on paper
And get it right—Tennessee sunlight,
Something by Vivaldi, rain on a Dublin street.
All these, and the self that carries the other around
And situates him for the work of his transported hand.
Let us sing, let us sing in Latin, let us stand
Up on elated feet and sing "Magnificat!"

Wake Me In South Galway

Wake me in South Galway, or better yet
In Clare. You'll know the pub I have in mind.
Improvise a hearse—one of those decrepit
Postal vans would suit me down to the ground—
A rust-addled Renault, Kelly green with a splash
Of Oscar Wilde yellow stirred in to clash
With the dazzling perfect meadows and limestone
On the coast road from Kinvara down toward Ballyvaughan.

Once you've got in off the road at Newquay
Push aside some barstools and situate me
Up in front by the door where the musicians sit,
Their table crowded with pints and a blue teapot,
A pouch of Drum, some rolling papers and tin
Whistles. Ask Charlie Piggott to play a tune
That sounds like loss and Guinness, turf smoke
and rain,
While Brenda dips in among the punters like a hedge-wren.

Will I hear it? Maybe not. But I hear it now.
The smoke of the music fills my nostrils, I feel the attuned
Box and fiddle in harness, pulling the plough
Of the melody, turning the bog-dark, root-tangled ground.
Even the ceramic collie on the windowsill
Cocks an ear as the tune lifts and the taut sail
Of the Galway hooker trills wildly in its frame on the wall,
Rippling to the salt pulse and sea breeze of a West Clare reel.

Many a night, two octaves of one tune,
We sat here side by side, your body awake
To a jig or slide, me mending the drift of a line
As the music found a path to my notebook.
Lost in its lilt and plunge I would disappear
Into the heathery freedom of a slow air

Or walk out under the powerful stars to clear
My head of thought and breathe their cooled-down fire.

When my own session ends, let me leave like that,
Porous to the wind that blows off the ocean.
Goodbye to the company and step into the night
Completed and one-off, like a well-played tune—
Beyond the purified essence of hearth fires
Rising from the life of the parish, past smoke and stars,
Released from everything I've done and known.
I won't go willingly, it's true, but I'll be gone.

We Kept Missing Each Other

Those nights I anchored the far end
of the bar at the Black Mariah,
      spilling drinks and feeding
         the jukebox with lugubrious quarters,
you'd be halfway up Mount Analogue
hooded in that weird white kaftan of yours,
sitting in the lotus mumbling your incomprehensible mantra,
inhaling moonlight through the business end of your kundalini.

But when I tried to join you, belaying up
a rubble-choked crevasse—
my knuckles bleeding, one knee out of whack—
I found the hut empty,
your devotional candle still a-smoulder.
Years later I heard you had something going on Wall Street,
were getting pretty good at puts and takes.

Myself, I was always shy around girls.
    You had if anything too many of them.
"A thirst for loving shook him like a snake," they quoted.
Porfirio Rubirosa just didn't
        measure up, they said.
The word Fred Astaire was mentioned.

We kept missing each other.
I was living on a commune in Venezuela
shrimping off a houseboat,
drift-fishing for sharks.
        You were cultivating the perfect lawn.
Your garage was in perfect order.
The wax job on your Buick was dazzling.

I paid off my debts, got a job
writing for The Wall Street Journal.
My rental properties were starting to pay off.
      That's when I found you working as a shade-tree mechanic
                              outside of Yuma, Arizona.
Brought you a six-pack of Pabst Blue Ribbon while you
rebuilt a Volkswagen engine on a riverbank under cottonwoods.

            I felt most at ease in a hotel,
liked putting my belongings into impersonal drawers.
      You were spending most of your time at home by this point,
smoking your pipe by the fire looking Victorian,
a paterfamilias surrounded by the next generation.

And just to think that Richard was your name too!

Notes

The first two lines of "The World Is" are borrowed, with her permission, from a poem by Paula Meehan.

Many details from "Legends of Lady FitzPigge-Hightits" are taken from Anne de Courcy's biography, *Circe: The Life of Edith Marchioness of Londonderry*. The poem, however, is a fiction.

"Habitat" is based on an article in the Kilcolgan, Co Galway, parish newsletter by the naturalist Gordon D'Arcy, and represents a collaboration between Mr. D'Arcy and the author.

"Osmanca" is the Turkish word which translates as "Ottoman," referring here to the older form of the Turkish language, before the modernizing reforms of the 20th century.

Biographical Note

Richard Tillinghast, who grew up in Memphis, is a graduate of Sewanee and Harvard, where he studied with Robert Lowell and later wrote a critical memoir, *Robert Lowell's Life and Work: Damaged Grandeur*. His *Selected Poems* came out in Ireland in 2010, and in 2010 he was awarded a Guggenheim Foundation Fellowship in poetry in addition to a National Endowment for the Arts Fellowship in translation for *Dirty August*, his versions of poems by the Turkish poet Edip Cansever, written in collaboration with his daughter, the poet Julia Clare Tillinghast. His 2012 travel book, *An Armchair Traveller's History of Istanbul*, published in London, was nominated for the Royal Society of Literature's Ondaatje Prize. He has taught at Harvard, Berkeley, Sewanee, and the University of Michigan, and is one of the founders of the Bear River Writers' Conference. The author of five works of creative nonfiction, his most recent publication is *Journeys into the Mind of the World: A Book of Places*, (2017). He has lived in Ireland as well as America, and now divides his time between Hawaii and a summer house in Sewanee, Tennessee.